The Law Commission

Working Paper No. 92

First published 1985

ISBN 0 11 730173 6

THE LAW COMMISSION

WORKING PAPER NO. 92

TRANSFER OF LAND

FORMALITIES FOR CONTRACTS FOR SALE ETC OF LAND

CONTENTS

FORMALITIES FOR CONTRACTS FOR SALE ETC. OF LAND

SUMMARY

In this Working Paper, the Property Law Team within the Law Commission examines, as part of the programme for the simplication of conveyancing, the formalities required for the sale or other disposition of land. The paper makes no provisional proposals of the Commission itself but outlines five suggestions: that there should be no substantial change in the present law (which requires at least written evidence); that in future no formalities should be required; that all such contracts should actually have to be in writing; that contracts for the sale of land would be in a prescribed form; or that there should be a "cooling off" period after an oral or written contract during which either party can withdraw. The purpose of the paper is to obtain the views not only of practitioners and other legal experts but also of the public.

THE LAW COMMISSION

ITEM IX OF THE FIRST PROGRAMME

TRANSFER OF LAND

FORMALITIES FOR CONTRACTS FOR SALE ETC OF LAND

PART I

INTRODUCTION

1.1 In 1965 in the First Programme of the Law Commission, which was approved by the Lord Chancellor, it was recommended "that an examination be made of the system of conveying unregistered land with a view to its modernisation and simplification". As part of that programme we have been considering contracts relating to sales and other dispositions of land or any interest in land.

1.2 The problem with which this paper is concerned is the extent to which the law should require any formalities to be observed in the formation of such contracts. At present a valid contract for the sale or other disposition of land can be made in the same way as a valid contract for the sale of any other property. However, by virtue of section 40 of the Law of Property Act 1925, it cannot be enforced by action unless either the person one wishes to sue or someone on his behalf has signed a written version of the contract or there is a sufficient act of part performance. The specific problems that have arisen in the interpretation of this section[1] are explained in some detail below. It is clear that doubts exist as to the proper interpretation of the section and for that reason alone it is suitable for consideration. More fundamentally we wish to examine whether there is any need for special rules for contracts relating to land, and whether they should relate to the way in which the contract is made, or to the way in which it becomes actionable.

1.3 It was after the case of Law v. Jones[2] that practitioners became aware of the fact that clients might have an oral agreement enforced against them by action notwithstanding that the only written evidence of it was a solicitor's letter marked "subject to contract"; i.e. such a letter was held by the Court of Appeal to be sufficient to fulfill the requirements of section 40. This "discovery" caused solicitors some understandable alarm[3] and this Commission was asked by The Law Society in 1973 to look at a proposed amendment to section 40 and to consider whether there was any better alternative. Numerous proposals were put forward in the immediate post-Law v. Jones period.

1.4 However, in another Court of Appeal case, Tiverton Estates Ltd v. Wearwell Ltd[4] it was held that, despite Law v. Jones, the words "subject to contract" used in a solicitor's letter would prevent it from being used against a client as evidence of an oral agreement. The court in the later case held that a section 40 memorandum must acknowledge a contract whilst the words "subject to contract" deny a contract. On the 12 February 1974, in response to a letter from the Commission as to whether our work was expected to continue in relation to The Law Society proposal, the Society said: "The Council consider that, following the decision in the case of Tiverton Estates Ltd. v. Wearwell Ltd. current conveyancing practice is now reasonably satisfactory." They went on to say, however, that reform of section 40 was still necessary.

1.5 In 1977 the Law Reform Committee took up the question of section 40 as "a worthwhile area of reform". They decided not to commence work on it however, because "the issues are not primarily legal, and the question has some political flavour ..." and they considered it "difficult to see quite how the present law could be improved." They suggested that the subject was more appropriate for the Law Commission.[5]

1.6 Section 40 remains a problem quite apart from Law v. Jones[6] and Tiverton Estates Ltd. v. Wearwell Ltd.[7] Criticisms of the section have been varied.[8] Each phrase has been the subject of litigation. The section has long appeared ripe for examination in the interests of modernisation and simplification of conveyancing, though "the question of how it shall be reformed is much more difficult and complex than whether it should be ..."[9]

1.7 The Government's Conveyancing Committee in its Second Report (1985) has recently noted a need for an examination of this aspect of the transaction.[10]

1.8 One further point when considering reform is that by clause 5 of the Administration of Justice Bill (1985) only qualified persons (as defined in the Solicitors Act 1974 as amended) will be able to prepare an instrument which is a contract for the sale or other disposition of land (except a contract to grant a short lease) in return for any fee, gain or reward. While this provision would not invalidate a contract in writing prepared by an unqualified person, it does mean that the vast majority of such contracts should be prepared either by qualified persons or by the parties themselves. Further, any reform which insists on the contract itself actually being in writing in all cases (as opposed to a minimum requirement of merely being evidenced in writing which is the case at present) will be seen to strengthen this provision. Alternatively any reform which relaxed requirements for writing would make this proposed provision (in clause 5) less effective.

PART II

EXISTING LAW

2.1 The following paragraphs purport to offer no more than a basic outline[1] of section 40 of the Law of Property Act 1925. For a detailed exposition of the problems raised by this section see Part III below. The section reads:

> "(1) No action may be brought upon any contract for the sale or other disposition of land or any interest in land, unless the agreement upon which such action is brought, or some memorandum or note thereof, is in writing, and signed by the party to be charged or by some other person thereunto by him lawfully authorised.
>
> (2) This section applies to contracts whether made before or after the commencement of this Act and does not affect the law relating to part performance, or sales by the court."

2.2 The Statute of Frauds 1677, from which section 40(1) is derived, was passed "For prevention of many fraudulent practices, which are commonly endeavoured to be upheld by perjury and subornation of perjury."[2] At the time when the Statute of Frauds was enacted neither the parties themselves nor anyone interested in the result of the action could give evidence. In these circumstances the potential frauds which might be perpetrated by one party who could call some outside oral evidence were obvious. Today these restrictions on the admissibility of evidence do not apply and the justification for what is now section 40(1) must therefore be sought on some other grounds.

2.3 Section 40(1) replaced part of section 4 of the Statute of Frauds 1677, which referred to "any contract or sale of lands, tenements and hereditaments, or any interest in or concerning them," and was intended to give effect to the construction placed on these words.[3] The remainder of section 4 of the 1677 Act (except for words referring, in effect, to contracts of guarantee), together with section 4 of the Sale of Goods Act 1893 (which had replaced section 17 of the 1677 Act and which concerned contracts for the sale of goods for £10 or more), was repealed in 1954[4] following recommendations made in 1937 by the Law Revision Committee appointed to report on the Statute of Frauds and the Doctrine of Consideration.[5] This Committee was not required to consider section 40 of the Law of Property Act 1925. Nevertheless it has been suggested that some of the Law Revision Committee's criticisms appear to be equally applicable to section 40[6] and thus the very existence of section 40 may be questioned as one of the last remnants of legal formalities which have otherwise disappeared.

2.4 The historical purpose of section 40 was to avoid parties being held to an alleged agreement the terms of which they had not in fact agreed. In practice, of course, it may also be used by a party to escape from a contract, and it is for this reason that problems have arisen "as the judges have wrestled with its interpretation in a valiant endeavour to enforce the bargain the parties have made."[7]

Contracts within section 40

2.5 Section 40 applies to any contract for the sale or other disposition of land or any interest in land, "land" being widely defined by section 205(1)(ix) of the Law of Property Act 1925.[8] The Court of Appeal said obiter in Cooper v. Critchley[9] that the section applied to contracts disposing of an interest under a trust for sale of land[10] (despite an express exclusion of an undivided share in land from the statutory definition of "land"). The phrase "other disposition of land" would include the granting of a lease, an option, mortgage etc.[11]

All material terms

2.6 It has become unclear whether or not the memorandum need acknowledge the existence of a contract[12] but it is not doubted that a sufficient memorandum must not deny the contract. Also, for any memorandum to satisfy the statute the parties must be so described that their identities could not fairly be disputed,[13] the physical property must be ascertainable[14] as also must be the price or other consideration.[15] Any other agreed or express terms (though not necessarily implied terms) must similarly be evidenced.[16]

Signature

2.7 Finally the memorandum must be signed by the party to be charged or by his "lawfully authorised" agent. The signature need not be a subscription at the foot of the agreement provided that it governs the whole memorandum; it may be merely initials or a printed name provided that the intention is to authenticate the document.[17] The contract can be enforced only against a party who, personally or by his agent, has signed a memorandum or note of it.

2.8 Since there is no statutory definition of "lawfully authorised", the ordinary principles of agency appear to be applicable. An agent may therefore sign on behalf of his principal if actual authority to do so has been expressly conferred upon him, or if it can properly be implied from the attendant circumstances. Additionally, although there is no clear authority to this effect, a signature within an agent's apparent or ostensible authority should suffice unless a court were to hold that section 40(1) refers only to actual authority.

Joinder of documents

2.9 If there is more than one document, then the two or more documents may be read together provided there is a reference in a signed one to the other or others.[18] An implicit reference has been considered sufficient.[19]

Non-compliance

2.10 As section 40 clearly states, non-compliance does not totally invalidate the contract but merely prevents an action for damages or a claim for specific performance. The contract may still be enforced otherwise than by a court action, in particular by forfeiture of any deposit paid under an oral contract upon default by a purchaser.[20]

2.11 It is perhaps not too obvious to mention that there must actually be a concluded contract before section 40 becomes an issue. Also it is clear that the statute must be specifically pleaded as a defence. Thus the section whilst not affecting the essential validity of the contract provides a procedural bar resembling those provided by the Limitation Act 1980.[21]

Part performance

2.12 The section expressly preserves the doctrine of part performance, so that even if there is no signed memorandum a contract may be enforceable if the plaintiff has carried out some or all of his obligations under the contract. The doctrine is based on the principle that equity will not allow a statute to be used as an instrument of fraud. To enforce a contract by means of the doctrine, the plaintiff must show that he has done such acts as indicate, on a balance of probabilities, that they had been performed in reliance on a contract which is consistent with the contract alleged to exist.[22] The acts need not be such as would demonstrate the precise terms of the contract. Not all acts done in the performance of a contract will be sufficient to raise an equity in favour of the plaintiff and so give him a remedy. However a number of acts and perhaps words joined together may "throw light on each other" and there is no good reason to exclude light.[23]

2.13 There are some limitations on the operation of the doctrine. There must be a contract in the first place, mere negotiations not being enough.[24] The doctrine can be used only to enforce oral contracts or those with insufficient writing to satisfy section 40(1); it cannot be used to supply omissions from a written contract. The most important limitation is that, as the doctrine is equitable, any remedy is in the discretion of the court albeit exercised in accordance with established principles; for example, the court will not intervene if the plaintiff has behaved inequitably, nor if he has an alternative equally effective common law remedy.[25]

2.14 The operation of the doctrine of part performance has fairly recently been re-examined by the House of Lords in Steadman v. Steadman.[26] In this case a husband and wife in proceedings following divorce entered into an oral agreement in relation to, inter alia, the matrimonial home of which they were joint owners. Mrs. Steadman agreed to surrender her interest in the house to her husband. In return he would pay her £1,500 plus £100 in full satisfaction of arrears of maintenance. Mr. Steadman duly paid the £100 and his solicitor prepared and delivered a deed of transfer for Mrs. Steadman to execute. She refused, and Mr. Steadman sought to enforce the oral agreement on the grounds of part performance. It was held that he had shown that he had acted to his detriment; that the acts indicated on a balance of probabilities that they had been performed in reliance on a contract consistent with the contract alleged; and that in the circumstances it would be inequitable to rely on a defence under section 40(1) and so oral evidence should be allowed to prove the contract, which was thus enforced against the wife.

2.15 The case raises a number of wider issues in relation to part performance generally. There was some disagreement amongst their Lordships as to whether the acts performed need indicate a contract relating to land.[27] Lord Salmon and Lord Morris were of the opinion that they should. Lord Reid and Viscount Dilhorne thought this unnecessary and Lord Simon thought it was unnecessary to decide the issue as there were such acts in the case. In the later case of Re Gonin[28] Walton J. took the view that the acts of the plaintiff must refer to the land, on the ground that this was in accord with established equitable jurisprudence.[29]

2.16 It had been thought that the payment of money alone could not be a sufficient act of part performance as it has no obvious or necessary connection with any contract. However it was clearly accepted in Steadman that payment of money can be an act of part performance, and Walton J. accepted this in Re Gonin. Payment of money will not always be sufficient, but the circumstances surrounding a payment of money may be such that the payment becomes evidence not only of the existence of the contract under which it was made but also of the nature of the contract.[30]

2.17 Finally it is clear that the acts of part performance by the husband in the case were considered sufficient even though they did not prove the exact terms of the contract. The acts no longer need to be "unequivocal" so long as they show that some contract has been made.[31]

PART III

PROBLEMS

3.1 Problems arising out of section 40 may be divided into two main groups:

A. Difficulties with interpretation of the statute itself, and

B. Difficulties raised by its interaction with part performance.

In addition there are certain general criticisms which have been made and mention will be made of these first.

3.2 Section 40 was not within the terms of reference of the 1937 Law Revision Committee when they considered the Statute of Frauds 1677.[1] Many of their criticisms have been said, however, to be equally applicable to section 40.[2] The criticisms were:[3]

(1) The requirement of a note in writing was introduced at a time when the parties themselves could not give evidence.[4]

(2) Besides shutting out perjury any such requirement also more frequently "shuts out the truth."

(3) ... [Clearly not applicable].

(4) Whether or not a party makes a note of the agreement/transaction is a matter of luck; therefore the requirement is "out of accord with the way business is normally done".[5]

(5) The operation of the requirement is often lopsided and partial. In a contract between A and B, if A has signed a sufficient memorandum but B has not, B can enforce the contract whereas A cannot.

(6) The section does not reduce contracts which do not comply with it to mere nullities but merely makes them unenforceable by action. This may lead to "anomalous results", the given example being Morris v. Baron.[6] There a contract which complied with section 4 of the 1677 Act was superseded by a second contract which did not. It was held that neither contract was enforceable: the earlier contract because it was rescinded by the later, and the later one because it failed to comply with the statute.[7]

These criticisms will be referred to further when certain proposals for reform are outlined.

A. Difficulties with Interpretation of the Statute

3.3 The meaning of "agreement" The most important issue under this heading has been and may still be that already referred to in Part I, namely the interpretation of the word "agreement". The word "agreement" may be said to have at least three meanings,[8] the fact of consensus, the terms of agreement, or a document which records the agreement.

3.4 In the case of Law v. Jones[9] it was held (Russell L.J. dissenting) that a sufficient section 40 memorandum need only record the terms agreed, also that the words "subject to contract" did not prevent there being a sufficient memorandum, for a firm agreement has the effect of "eliminating any qualifying effect which the presence of the words may have had ..."[10]. In the case of Tiverton Estates v. Wearwell,[11] however, a differently constituted Court of Appeal reached a contrary decision, that is, that the writing relied upon must acknowledge the existence of a contract and that the words "subject to contract" constitute a denial.

3.5 Despite the fact that these cases are "undoubtedly in conflict"[12] and the fact that it has been strongly argued[13] that the Tiverton case cannot, on grounds of precedent, be taken to overrule Law v. Jones, it is true to say that the Tiverton case often appears to be accepted as deciding the law.[14]

3.6 Buckley L.J. may well have been correct in saying in Law v. Jones[15] that section 40 "presupposes the existence of a contract and in case after case in the books one finds the existence of the contract established by extraneous evidence." However, it does not follow from this that the existence of an agreement can be contradicted or doubted in the memorandum.[16]

3.7 Which opinion is correct, however, is almost irrelevant for present purposes since any doubt as to such a crucial point is ground enough for reform. Despite The Law Society's claim that, following the Tiverton case, this aspect of conveyancing practice is reasonably satisfactory, the problem, as we have indicated, remains. Indeed The Law Society itself stressed the continuing need for reform of section 40.[17]

3.8 "Or any interest in land". Another problem arising with the words of the statute is the proper interpretation of the phrase "or any interest in land". Although "an undivided share in land" is expressly excluded from the wide definition of land in section 205(1)(ix) of the Law of Property Act 1925, section 40(1) has been obiter, said to apply to a contract for the sale of an undivided share in land.[18] Therefore an interest once considered to be a mere interest in the proceeds of sale[19] must now be treated as an interest in land. This treatment has moreover been accepted without argument by both the Court of Appeal and the House of Lords in Steadman v. Steadman.[20]

3.9 Other contracts which have been held to fall within section 40 as concerning "land or any interest in land" include a contract for the sale of debentures charged on land[21] and a right to shoot and take away game.[22]

3.10 Land includes fixtures which have become part of the "land", so that a contract for their sale or other disposition is thus within section 40 even when sold separately from the land.[23] Problems with the definition of land in general are also applicable with section 40, for example the distinction between a lease and a licence and the question of whether an irrevocable licence is yet an interest in land.[24] These problems are not peculiar to section 40 however, and will not be discussed further here.

3.11 Judicial construction As the section was intended to prevent fraud, the judiciary have naturally been loath to allow the lack of a sufficient memorandum to defeat an otherwise established contract. A number of extensions or exceptions have therefore been devised, aside from the doctrine of part performance, to enable or facilitate the enforcement of contracts. The operation and availability of these is not always clear.

3.12 Joinder of documents First there is what might be described as the joinder rule.[25] It is clear that the Interpretation Act 1978, s. 6(c), provides for singular words in statutes to include the plural. However, not all such words will be so read.[26] Nevertheless, even if more than one document was envisaged by the phrase "memorandum or note" in section 40, the courts have allowed plaintiffs to adduce parol evidence to explain and connect incomplete documents until a complete memorandum is collected.[27] An implied reference may suffice for this, if a number of documents when placed side by side are seen to refer to the same transaction.[28] Not all the documents need to be signed if the reference to the same transaction is "manifest".[29]

3.13 In the case of Timmins v. Moreland Street Property Co. Ltd.[30] Jenkins L.J. stated that in order to join two or more documents, one of the documents must be signed and must contain "some reference, express or implied, to some other document or transaction". After reaching the conclusion that a cheque was only evidence of "the mere fact that the payment must have been made for some purpose or for some consideration", he said that it could not "reasonably be held to amount to a reference to some other document or transaction within the principle ... stated". The dicta of Jenkins L.J. in the Timmins case have recently been approved by the Privy Council in Elias v. George Sahely & Co. (Barbados) Ltd.[31]

3.14 While in any particular case it may seem entirely reasonable to allow the joinder of documents, the development of the rule has added to the uncertainty in the application of section 40. It may be difficult to know in any particular case whether there has been a sufficient reference in one document to another to permit joinder, and the extent to which the courts will allow extrinsic evidence to be used to prove the connection between two documents is unclear.

3.15 Identification of parties, property, price Further problems have been caused by the fact that oral evidence has been allowed in order to identify the parties to an agreement where their names are not stated, or are stated incorrectly.[32] Thus a memorandum in which a party is mentioned by capacity but not by name may suffice.[33] Nevertheless a description which is too indefinite will not suffice as the parties will not be considered to be ascertainable (e.g. "my clients", in Lovesy v. Palmer[34]).

3.16 In relation to the parties this may not be an exception to the requirements of section 40 for, as Lord Evershed M.R. said in Davies v. Sweet.[35]

> "The statutory language requires that there should be a sufficient note or memorandum of the contract alleged, that is of its essential provisions. It does not in terms require that the contracting parties should be named or identified ..."

Consistently with this a memorandum may be sufficient where it does not actually identify one of the parties and yet does identify an agent who will be bound by the agreement through incurring personal liability.[36]

3.17 The property and price, however, are terms of the agreement and yet they too need only be ascertainable, not necessarily ascertained. The question is one of construction. "[T]wenty-four acres of land, freehold, at Totmonslow" was held to be a sufficiently certain description of the property in the case of Plant v. Bourne.[37] The court will assume that a man is selling his own property.[38] It will only be necessary for the property to be defined in a physical sense as, without mention of the interest being disposed of, it is implied that an unencumbered freehold is to pass.[39] Similarly an agreement to sell at a fair and reasonable valuation will be valid and enforceable as a court is capable of determining such price[40] by substituting its own machinery for that agreed by the parties. This will not be the case where the valuation machinery was of the essence. However, where no price is agreed, the court will not imply a term that a reasonable price must be paid.[41] It is important to remember in each of these cases that where a term is not certain, this will result not only in there being an unenforceable contract but in there being no contract to be enforced.

3.18 Signature The courts have perhaps been least rigid with regard to the requirement in section 40 that the memorandum be "signed" by the party charged. Names merely printed in the memorandum (or indeed initials) may be sufficient signature where the party writes them or otherwise indicates his agreement,[42] although printed names or initials will not suffice where the memorandum shows that they were not inserted as a signature, as, for example, where at the conclusion of an agreement the words "As witness our hands" were written with no signature following.[43] However there may be uncertainty in any particular case as to whether a name or initials will be accepted as a signature.[44]

3.19 Quite apart from the difficulties as to what constitutes a signature, there may be a question as to whether a document has been properly signed if the document has been altered. It has been held that where a written contract is altered subsequently to signature, an oral approval of the alteration will revive the signature only in cases where the variation is to rectify an inaccurate formulation and not where it is a variation by consent of a concluded agreement.[45] Although Goulding J. felt constrained to accept this "illogical distinction", it has since been argued[46] that the distinction is supported neither by the authority relied upon in that case nor by principle. In light of this, problems may arise in practice where due initialling of alterations is overlooked, or is not insisted upon, for example in the common situation where the completion date is only agreed after exchange of contracts: strictly speaking, without initialling, there will be no "signed" contract or memorandum.

3.20 Waiver of a term or submission to omissions

It is clear from the wording of section 40 that what is required is a memorandum of the agreement actually made between the parties. However the courts have allowed contracts to be enforced even though the memorandum does not contain all the terms of the agreement if, first, the term omitted is solely for the benefit of the plaintiff and, secondly, the plaintiff decides to waive the term.[47] The plaintiff will have to establish that there was a concluded contract and that the term was not "really an essential part of the bargain."[48]

3.21 Whether the converse is true, that is, if an omitted term is to the detriment of one party exclusively, that party may submit to its performance and then enforce the contract as evidenced by the memorandum, is perhaps more doubtful. The rule was adopted by Williams on Vendor and Purchaser[49] on the basis of the decision in Martin v. Pycroft.[50] However a contrary result was reached by Harman J. in Burgess v. Cox.[51] This case was in turn not followed in Scott v. Bradley[52] where Plowman J. followed Martin v. Pycroft in preference to Harman J's decision. In this latest case a plaintiff was held entitled to specific performance by submitting to perform the missing term that he pay half the defendant's costs.

3.22 Summary Waiver of terms, joinder of documents, acceptance of printed signatures and the other matters mentioned all appear to derive from attempts by the courts to prevent the section from being used, in effect, as an instrument of fraud: the primary example of this approach was, of course, the doctrine of part performance which is now recognised in section 40(2). The result has been that the Act has "acquired a thick crustation of legal authority and judicial gloss, much of it inconsistent and unsupported by the enactment itself."[53] The law on the matter is no longer codified within the statute but must be deduced from judgments, and doubts will inevitably exist as to the present scope and future application of section 40(1).

B. Problems with Part Performance. Is Section 40(1) a Dead Letter?

3.23 It has been said that "If ... one party to an oral contract can render it enforceable by his own unilateral act without the defendant's assent, then it is indeed difficult to resist the conclusion that s.40(1) has been judicially repealed, so opening the door wide to the evils it was designed to avoid".[54] This result is attributed to the decision in Steadman v. Steadman.[55] In that case, the House of Lords re-examined the question of what acts amount to part performance, and held that mere payment of a sum of money in the circumstances of the case amounted to a sufficient act of part performance so that the contract was enforceable despite the lack of writing. Further, the majority of the law lords severally indicated that, in the ordinary circumstances of a contract for the sale of land, a sufficient such act could be found in the fact of the purchaser instructing solicitors to prepare and submit a draft conveyance or transfer. In consequence, it appears that an oral contract for sale can readily and unilaterally be rendered enforceable by the purchaser.[56] It has similarly been suggested that a vendor might rely on the unilateral act of (part) performance constituted by actually executing a deed of conveyance or transfer.[57] However, the precise position is not entirely clear for it has been argued[58] to the contrary that the only innovations in the Steadman case were the lowering of the standard of proof and allowing the payment of money to be an act of part performance.

3.24 In that case there was no discussion of any requirement that the defendant should have knowledge of, and acquiesce in, the plaintiff's acts amounting to part performance. On the facts of the case it may perhaps be assumed that there was in fact knowledge, since the sending of a document for execution after the making of a contract is a part of normal conveyancing practice. The point was, however, not canvassed and the question of whether the defendant's acquiescence is relevant was therefore left open.

3.25 A point which was canvassed but still left open was whether or not acts of part performance must indicate merely a contract of the type alleged or rather indicate a contract relating to land.[59] Walton J. in Re Gonin[60] regarded the doctrine of part performance as including an evidential factor, so that the acts relied upon must themselves be indicative of a contract concerning land. This view has been criticised.[61]

3.26 The decision in Steadman v. Steadman has left the scope of the doctrine of part performance in a very uncertain state. Any consideration of section 40 will have to address itself to this problem, and not just to the, perhaps better known, problems of section 40(1).

PART IV

EARLIER PROPOSALS

All contracts in writing

4.1 One suggestion, made shortly after the decisions in Law v. Jones and Tiverton,[1] was that the words "or some memorandum or note thereof" should be deleted from section 40(1). The effect of this amendment would be that for contracts for the sale or other disposition of land to be enforceable by action, the agreement would have to be "in writing". The following questions, it has been put to us, may be raised when considering the suggestion:

(a) If a contract concerning land has to be in writing, how far is it necessary to define the essential terms?

(b) Ought an agent to have implied authority to sign such a contract?

(c) Should section 40 be retained at all for dispositions other than sales of land?

(d) Would it be possible to read two or more documents together to satisfy the requirement?

(e) Would the "latent but nevertheless real problems that exist as to what 'Conditions of Sale' apply .... be greatly aggravated"?[2]

(f) Can such a radical departure from settled rules as to the formation of contracts be justified?

(g) Would it be advisable to add a qualification such as "save where it would be inequitable for the defendant to plead this provision"?

4.2 We shall refer to this suggestion further below as one of the options for reform. However it should be noticed also that the distinction between a contract in writing and one which is evidenced in writing may not always be clear[3]. Also it should be appreciated that the mere deletion of the words "or some note or memorandum thereof" would not produce a requirement that the contract must be in writing in order to be valid: an oral contract, as now, would not be void but simply unenforceable by action.

Abolition of part performance

4.3 Coupled with the above suggestion was one for the repeal of section 40(2) and the abolition of part performance. Again we consider this proposal further below. However it should be noted that merely repealing section 40(2) would not abolish the doctrine of part performance. The sub-section is merely there for the avoidance of doubt.

"Subject to contract"

4.4 Two suggestions were made[4] which would solve the specific problem as to the effect for present purposes of the use of the words "subject to contract". One was that section 40(1) should be amended to include the words "which recognises the existence of the contract" (i.e. between "some memorandum or note thereof" and "is in writing"). Alternatively the words "which does not deny the contract" could be inserted and a new provision introduced to the effect that if the words "subject to contract" appear in a document, it would not be possible to say that that stipulation had been waived.

4.5 In similar vein it may be suggested that all agreements for the sale of land be deemed to be made "subject to contract" unless or until it was expressly agreed in writing to the contrary. Auction sales and sales by tender would have to be exempt from this requirement.

4.6 Our present view is that these three suggestions would solve too specific a problem without dealing with the more general problems created by section 40. For that reason we are not making proposals based on them, nor will we discuss them further. Nevertheless we would welcome comments on them.

Authority to sign

4.7 There is a particular problem of a note or memorandum evidencing a contract being signed inadvertently by a solicitor or other agent before a party intended the contract to become enforceable. This is due to the fact that the authority need not actually be to enter into a contract or to make a contract enforceable but may merely be to sign the document (e.g. a letter or receipt) which happens to constitute sufficient evidence of the contract.[5] The problem could be alleviated by providing that an agent must be specifically authorised in writing to sign the note or memorandum, if he is to be "lawfully authorised" within the section.[6] This should not make the disposition of land in practice slower than it is now, since in the ordinary case the contract will be in writing signed by the parties themselves.

Repeal of section 40

4.8 The attractively simple proposal has frequently been put forward that no special formalities should be required and that section 40 should be repealed and not replaced. The reasons usually given for this proposal are that the criticisms of formalities for other contracts made by the Law Revision Committee[7] apply equally to section 40 and that it is because section 40 is unnecessary that so much judicial interpretation has occurred. We consider this proposal further below as one of the options for reform.

Prescribed form

4.9 Another proposal which we consider further below is that there should be a prescribed form for contracts within section 40.[8] The form would contain the essential terms of the contract and a warning about the dangers of signing without advice. It could also contain some of the conditions of sale.

PART V

PRESENT PROPOSALS

5.1 In this Part we put forward for consideration five possible reforms of the law relating to the formalities for contracts for the sale or other disposition of interests in land. While this paper does end with a provisional conclusion we would like to emphasise that that is by no means a final conclusion and that we would like to receive views on all five proposals, and indeed, as to any others that we have not considered. Until we can gain some idea as to which proposals, if any, are likely to prove acceptable, it seems premature to go into great detail. We do not deny that some of the problems identified with respect to section 40 (for example, the precise extent to which joinder of documents is permitted) could arise in some of the proposals. However, we would hope to take account of these when making more detailed proposals at a later date. Before putting these proposals forward, we outline certain general principles which we consider must be taken into account in any reform of this area. We also discuss two questions, the answers to which will affect the approach to be taken.

General principles

5.2 We consider that there are three general principles which must be taken into account so far as possible in any reform in this area.

(i) No reform should increase the likelihood of contracts for the sale (or other disposition) of land becoming binding before the parties have been able to obtain legal advice.[1] This is not to say, however, that any reform should itself result in formalities which can only be undertaken by lawyers and not, for example, by the parties themselves if they so decide.

(ii) Any reform if unable to reduce the risk of injustice should at least not increase it. In particular, the imposition of any formal requirements should not be so inflexible that hardship or unfairness is perceived in cases of minor non-compliance.

(iii) Any reform should simplify or at least not complicate conveyancing. Although this is an argument for reducing formalities, so containing professionals' fees and assisting "do-it-yourself" conveyancers, certainty and reliability are often essential in dealings with land and may call for extra formalities.

Is land different?

5.3 The question of whether land should be treated differently from other property is important, and one which deserves serious consideration. There are many other forms of property which may be worth far more than a piece of land, yet no formalities are required for contracts relating to them. If one can contract to buy or sell £1 million pounds' worth of shares without formality, why should even the smallest interest in land require any contractual formality? One reason conventionally given is that land has the particular characteristic that many people may acquire interests in or over one piece of land. For this reason, it is said, some formality must be required in dealings with land if confusion is not to arise as to whom owns what. From this point of view section 40(1) is obviously linked with the other sections of the Law of Property Act 1925 which require formalities for dealings with land.[2] While we find this argument persuasive in relation to the completion of contracts, i.e. the actual creation of interests in land, even then it may not be totally compelling, because some third party interests can be created in other forms of property. More persuasive is the point that in principle each particular piece of land is unique, so that for contracts relating to land the important remedy of specific performance is much more likely to be available.

5.4 Another convincing argument, in our view, is that while there are other forms of property as valuable as land, for example, a Rolls Royce motorcar, most people do not deal in such property. For most people, the most significant transaction they will ever enter into is one relating to land, in particular the sale or purchase of a dwelling house. From this point of view, insisting on some formalities for the sale or purchase of land can be seen as a form of consumer protection for ordinary people who are engaged in a transaction which they will enter into only a few times in their lifetime, and which will often involve them in major financial commitments. However, the consumer protection approach is obviously not so appropriate for business transactions, for example, contracts for the grant of leases of commercial premises.

5.5 On balance, it is our provisional view that contracts for the sale of land should still be treated differently. However, others may well take a different view and this may have implications for the reform of the other sections of the Law of Property Act 1925 referred to above.

Formalities for what?

5.6 The other question which has general relevance to our proposals is whether, if formalities are required, they should be necessary so as to constitute a contract, or only to prove a contract. At present there can be a valid contract, which may be enforceable otherwise than by action, even if section 40(1) has not been complied with. One problem with this is that the question whether there is a contract at all tends to become entwined with questions as to whether the formalities have been observed. Part performance may also be used to enforce a valid, but informal, contract, giving rise to difficult questions as to the proper scope of that doctrine. Against this, to insist that contracts must actually be made in some formal way creates certainty: the formalities either have or have not been observed. That certainty may, however, be achieved at the expense of occasional hardship and apparent unfairness if the parties have genuinely reached an agreement which is then invalidated for lack of a mere formality.

5.7 Again we seek views on this issue. However, our provisional view is that the additional certainty is, in this area, worth the risk of some unfairness. It seems likely to us that most people know that dispositions of land involve some formality and indeed lawyers are nearly always instructed to act for the parties. The distinction at present made between valid but unenforceable contracts, on the one hand, and invalid contracts, on the other hand, is probably not well understood. Where the parties have acted in ignorance of the legal formalities it is probably preferable for any contract to be void, rather than for there to be a contract which is valid but enforceable by some means and not others and possibly enforceable against one party but not against the other. However, to adopt the maxim that certainty is the next best thing to justice would, in this context, involve a substantial change from the present judicial attitude.

5.8 Consultees and other readers should appreciate that where an anticipated contract is void because not made in accordance with statutory formalities, it does not follow that the parties will simply be left remediless by the law. Apart altogether from any possibilities there may be of suing for damages in tort (e.g. deceit or negligence), either of the parties would where appropriate be able to seek restitution.[3] Thus if money has been paid as a deposit or part of the price by a prospective purchaser, recovery would generally be permitted because there would be a total failure of consideration.[4] Again, if work had been carried out on the land in anticipation of the contract by either of the parties, a quantum meruit claim might be made, in effect, for what the work is worth.[5] In addition to any common law remedies, some significant equitable intervention would not be ruled out. In particular, the doctrines of "promissory estoppel" and "proprietary estoppel" respectively might be applicable: these operate, in essence, where one person (A) has acted to his detriment and another person (B) was responsible for this - under the former doctrine, B will be precluded from resiling from his promise or representation, whilst under the latter doctrine, B will be precluded from denying A's supposed rights in B's property.[6] In the present context, the most likely sort of case again will be of improvements to land by a prospective purchaser carried out with the acquiescence at least of the prospective vendor. The nature of the equitable relief given will vary with the circumstances between reimbursement of cost or value of the improvements, this being secured sometimes by a lien or charge on the land, and actual conferment of the anticipated estate or interest in the land.[7] It appears to us obviously out of the question to exclude the application of these general judicial doctrines (restitution as well as equitable estoppel) in this particular area of sales etc. of land. Equally, it is thought inappropriate to attempt to spell out and perhaps circumscribe the requirements and limits of these still developing doctrines simply for present purposes or even to consider special extensions or restrictions. Nevertheless, the fact of their existence and development, as of many other relevant rules of law and equity, should be borne in mind when views are expressed as to any proposals that certain formalities should be necessary for the validity of a contract.

Proposal I

5.9 To make no change It is a tenable view that the existing law has caused only occasional difficulties and is in general well enough understood, and therefore that the present position should be retained with a minimum of necessary amendments or improvements. For example, if the doctrine of part performance is considered to be unclear or too wide, legislation could be used to clarify and circumscribe its scope. In addition, the word "agreement" in section 40(1) could be replaced or defined so that its interpretation did not depend on resolving judicial conflict in the Court of Appeal. Similarly, the limits of the joinder of documents principle, and the interpretation of the word "signed", could equally be spelt out by statute if thought necessary. This, however, might be thought a piecemeal approach whilst the various problems with the existing law which we have discussed show a prima facie case for an overall reform.

Proposal II

5.10 Repeal of section 40 without replacement This proposal would leave it open to the parties to establish the existence of a contract for the sale or other disposition of an interest in land by whatever evidence they could adduce. It has the advantage that, in the event of dispute, argument would focus on the substantive issue of whether there was a contract and not on the formal issue of whether there was a sufficient memorandum and signature. Most contracts would in practice almost certainly continue to be in writing and, of course, most contracts do not lead to a dispute. Most people nowadays know well enough not to enter into an oral agreement for the sale of land except "subject to contract" usually expressly but perhaps impliedly in the circumstances.[8] Arguably, therefore, the present formal requirements foster disputes by giving a party an opportunity to deny a contract which has actually been made and could otherwise be proved. If a need for protection against over-hasty oral contracts were felt, it might be achieved by providing a "cooling-off" period (see further para. 5.30).

5.11 However, we do not now recommend this proposal because it does not comply with the principles we have outlined above. It provides no means of encouraging the parties to take legal advice and it does nothing to prevent fraud. People might find themselves bound by a contract to buy or sell land without realising it. We have already explained why contracts concerning interests in land can be regarded as a special case. In addition, it would appear contrary to the principle otherwise adopted by the 1925 legislation of insisting that most matters or dispositions affecting title to land should involve writing.[9] That said, there might be advantages in adopting this proposal for contracts for the sale or other disposition of some interests in land where the principles outlined have less force. Where short leases[10] are concerned it may well appear anomalous that the lease itself can be granted orally, but a contract to grant such a lease requires writing. Short leases are excluded from clause 5 of the Administration of Justice Bill 1985[11] and similarly there may be a case for excluding them from any provisions for formalities. However, we are aware that contracts for short leases may prove as important for landowners as long leases in the light of the Rent Acts and other provisions for security of tenure.

Proposal III

5.12 All contracts relating to land to be in writing We have already discussed the advantages and disadvantages of making the formalities relate to the formation of the contract rather than the evidence required to prove it. Despite the questions raised, we tentatively favour a provision that contracts for the sale or other disposition of land should be in writing in order to be valid (i.e. not merely enforceable). Failure to put the agreement in writing would mean that there would be no contract at all. It seems to us that such a rule would have much to recommend it. At present lack of writing renders an otherwise binding contract unenforceable in the courts as a procedural or evidential bar, and this often seems draconian, hence the judicial attempts to minimise the impact of section 40. If there is clearly no contract at all without writing and if this is a matter of common knowledge, the law may be more acceptable.

5.13 It could be that it would be going too far to say that all contracts for the sale or other disposition of any interest in land should be in writing. We have already commented that it might be appropriate not to require any formalities for contracts for short leases. It may be that there are other contracts (for example contracts relating to equitable interests[12]) which should be excluded from such a provision. Alternatively, the requirement of being in writing could be confined to "estate contracts", i.e. a contract to convey or create a legal estate of the sort which can be protected by registration.[13] Note, however, that the statutory definition of "legal estate" is not at present restricted to legal freeholds and leases but covers, for example, easements and mortgages.[14] Again short leases could easily be excluded.[15] One advantage of confining the requirement to legal estates would be the avoidance of any need to dispute the precise meaning of an interest in land (e.g. where there is a licence or a share in the proceeds of salė). We would be glad to receive views on these alternatives.

5.14 If such a rule requiring contracts to be in writing in order to be validly made were introduced, then the doctrine of part performance would cease to operate in so far as contracts affected by the rule were concerned. Part performance only operates to permit the enforcement of an otherwise unenforceable but valid contract. If there is no valid contract, there can be no part performance. As has been shown the scope of the doctrine is far from certain, and from that point of view its exclusion would be an advantage. Against this it is unacceptable if a statute is being used as an instrument of fraud, and there is clearly a danger that a rule such as this would be used to escape from otherwise concluded agreements. There are two answers to this. One is that to make use of the provisions of a statute should not <u>of itself</u> be considered to be fraudulent, even in equity.[16] Secondly, the fact that the doctrine of part performance can no longer operate does not mean that will be completely without remedies: see the introduction to this Part where the possibilities of judicial intervention are outlined.[17]

5.15 Another issue which requires consideration is what has to be in writing: all the terms? or only the main terms? and if the latter how are they to be defined? Simply providing that the contract should be "in writing" without qualification would presumably call for all the terms agreed to be included, and would appear to be in line with existing provisions in the property legislation.[18] However it could cause injustice to continue to insist on all the agreed terms being in writing, because then a contract would be invalidated by the omission of one comparatively unimportant term. Accordingly, we would at present favour a provision that the main terms only should have to be in writing and that parol evidence should be allowed to prove any other agreed terms.[19] There would obviously be formidable difficulties in the way of formulating a statutory definition of main terms in the sense of the material or important provisions of each individual contract. However, it would appear possible to define main terms for present purposes in a bare minimum way so as to refer to the type of transaction (e.g. sale, exchange, lease, option, mortgage), the parties, the property concerned and the consideration. Equally, more detail might be called for in specified contracts. In the case of a lease, for example, perhaps it should be provided that the length of term, the rent and the date of commencement must be stated in writing as main terms.[20] We would very much welcome views as to what other terms, if any, should be included in such a provision. It may perhaps be helpful to remember during this exercise that any increase in the list of what is to be in writing (as opposed to being proved by parol evidence) will carry with it the greater risk of terms being left out by mistake and the whole contract therefore failing.

5.16 A requirement that the contract should be in writing would have other advantages over the present rule allowing subsequent written evidence of an oral contract. Not only would the writing have to embody the agreement but it would have to come into existence at the time of the alleged contract. Accordingly there could be no question of later letters, with or without the words "subject to contract", being sufficient. Nor, presumably, would a written offer accepted orally any longer suffice.[21] However, a contract by correspondence, that is by exchange of letters, ought to be good enough,[22] as also, of course, would be the present prevailing practice of making the contract by exchanging identical parts signed by the respective parties. It is assumed that the "joinder of documents" doctrine would, unless excluded by legislation, be equally applicable where the contract has to be in writing as it is now where only evidence in writing is required.[23] However, this leads to the question of signatures: who should be required to sign a contract in writing? It could be, as in section 40(1), only the defendant, the party to be charged, (or his agent), but this would seem quite inapt when the issue is the validity rather than the enforceability of the contract. It could be the vendor (or other grantor) alone, which would be in line with other statutory provisions for signature by the person creating or conveying an interest in land.[24] Or it could, better in our opinion, be by all the parties to the contract. Plainly agents should be permitted to sign on behalf of the parties. Although it would be possible to restrict this to "persons thereunto lawfully authorised in writing"[25] it might appear preferable to let the ordinary principles of agency operate.

Proposal IV

5.17 Prescribed form This proposal is a development of the previous one, since it is a proposal that the contract should not merely have to be in writing but should have to be in a particular prescribed form. What advantages would a prescribed form have over a simple requirement of writing?

(i) It would be completely clear whether a contract had been made or, at least, it would be clear when a contract has not been made. If there is only a requirement of writing there may be argument as to whether, e.g., an exchange of letters setting out the terms is sufficient.

(ii) A prescribed form could be used to carry warnings regarding the danger of entering into such a contract without first obtaining legal, financial or other advice.

(iii) The prescribed form could incorporate certain standard conditions of sale. Some of these might be incapable of exclusion.[26] Others could be varied by agreement. Generally the result should be much greater certainty as to the terms of the contract.

5.18 The idea of prescribing a format is far from a novel one in English law, such forms having been prescribed for hire purchase transactions for some time.[27] Similarly notices to quit dwellings are not valid unless they contain "such information as may be prescribed."[28] More relevant, perhaps, is the fact that forms have long been prescribed for dealings with registered land.[29]

5.19 The Second Report of the Government's Conveyancing Committee[30] has strongly recommended the use of a prescribed form for house transfers. It says:

> "There should be considered the suggestion for a statutorily prescribed form of contract for domestic conveyancing which would embody certain material terms, imply other terms subject to exclusion or variation, and be used in conjunction with a standard set of statutory conditions of sale. The necessary statute could be a new Sale of Land Act which would prescribe the form of contract and in addition replace with appropriate modernisation the existing relevant statutory provisions and codify the applicable rules of common law and equity. Recommendations for this reform should be undertaken as a matter of urgency by the Conveyancing Standing Committee or the Law Commission."

The suggestion referred to was elaborated in the body of the Report as follows:

> "7.7. Accordingly, an effective solution appeared to some to be a statutorily prescribed form of contract, use of which would be essential for validity as well as enforceability. This solution would incidentally by-pass many of the difficulties occasioned by the use or non-use of 'subject to contract' in relation to oral agreements as to price. The statute could inter alia (i) stipulate the material terms which must be agreed and embodied in the form; (ii) imply other terms subject to exclusion or variation; (iii) provide for void terms and terms which cannot be excluded or varied, or only excluded or varied subject to a reasonableness test; (iv) incorporate a standard set of statutory conditions of sale which could be promulgated by rules and up-dated from time to time; (v) cater for oral evidence of ancillary matters or as to chattels; (vi) deal with the requirement of signatures or other authentication by solicitors or other conveyancers on behalf of the parties; (vii) direct itself towards the implications of electronic communications; and (viii) require the setting out, principally for lay persons (e.g. 'do-it-yourself' conveyancers), of warning and other notes as to the manner and consequence of completing and signing the form."[31]

5.20 In this connection, it would appear highly desirable for there to be drafted an up-dated version of the Statutory Conditions of Sale published by the

Lord Chancellor under section 46 of the Law of Property Act 1925.[32] This version which should amalgamate the better aspects of The Law Society's, the National, and any other commercial sets of conditions of sale in present use, ought to be made of general application - rather than confined to contracts by correspondence (especially given the narrow definition of such contracts in the case of Stearn v. Twitchell[33]). The drafting could be undertaken in due course by the Standing Committee on Conveyancing originally suggested by the Royal Commission on Legal Services in 1979 and more recently endorsed by the Government's Conveyancing Committee.

5.21 The point that a prescribed form could be used to warn a layman against an unwise or hasty transaction is primarily valid so far as domestic conveyancing is concerned, although, for example, people taking assignments of leases of small shops may be equally at risk. It may be difficult to incorporate the terms of commercial transactions into a standard form. We do especially seek views on the question as to whether, if a prescribed form is thought acceptable, it should be restricted to domestic conveyancing. If that is a desirable proposition, it may still be difficult to find a suitable definition of "domestic". The First Report of the Government's Conveyancing Committee, when discussing the work to be done by licensed conveyancers, defined domestic conveyancing as "the sale, purchase or mortgage of a dwelling house, or part of a dwelling house, freehold or leasehold, and the gardens or yards (including garages or outhouses) enjoyed and occupied therewith".[34]

5.22 Similarly we seek views as to whether this prescribed form proposal should cover contracts for all kinds of transactions relating to land, e.g. dispositions of equitable interests;[35] disclaimers, releases, charges or mortgages. As with Proposal IV we would suggest excluding short leases, but perhaps all commercial leases and other transactions should be excluded as well. It may be that excluding certain kinds of transactions would be a better way of restricting the scope of the proposal than trying to find a suitable definition of "domestic conveyancing".

5.23 It is the present opinion within the Commission that if this proposal is adopted, it should be restricted to sales of land but <u>not</u> to domestic conveyancing. This is partly because this latter concept would be difficult to define and would involve borderline cases, but also because no harm will come from "warning" or "advising" in commercial cases, albeit often unnecessarily.

5.24 What terms should be in the prescribed form? Should there be one form, or (if not restricted to sales of land) a different form for each type of transaction? The fewer the terms in the prescribed form, the more practicable it will be to use it for different types of transaction. It should necessarily include the nature of the agreement, the parties, the property concerned, and the consideration. We would also suggest that it should incorporate statutory conditions of sale, most if not all of which would be variable by agreement stated in the prescribed form. Parol evidence would be allowed to prove other terms although these could for convenience be inserted in the form. So far as possible it would appear desirable to avoid a proliferation of forms. We would be anxious to avoid, so far as possible, the risks of contracts failing through inadvertent use of the wrong form. In this connection, hard cases turning on technicalities should be discouraged by envisaging the use of forms "substantially to the like effect" as those prescribed or even by giving the court jurisdiction to condone omissions where "just and equitable".[36]

5.25 Also to be taken into account, in considering this proposal, is the difficulty that some of the contracts in question will be "embedded" in other transactions, themselves embodied in documents, which might make the adoption of a particular form inappropriate or at least highly inconvenient. (Examples are: a partnership agreement containing an agreement as to the disposal of partnership premises on a change of partners; a company takeover agreement, making express provision relating to the business premises concerned; a lease containing an option to acquire the freehold reversion.) However this might not be thought an insuperable difficulty in practice: compare the prescribed forms for transfers of registered land[37] which are not infrequently incorporated by annexation into documents effecting larger transactions.

5.26 It might be beneficial to provide expressly that a contract in the prescribed form would become binding when signed by both parties,[38] even though one or other party had added "subject to contract" (or even substantially similar words) to the form.[39] If in two parts, contracts would be exchanged and become binding in the usual way. This would not prevent the parties from entering into a conditional contract, for example, one subject to planning permission for a particular development being obtained within a specified time. As is the case at present, problems of construction may occur when it is difficult to decide whether there is an agreed condition or term of a concluded contract or only a condition precedent to the formation of any contract.[40]

5.27 If such a prescribed form is to be the only method of forming a contract relating to land, then provision ought to be made as to variations of or additions to such contracts. This gives rise to obvious questions. Should oral variations or additions be allowed? If not must variations or additions be made in writing? Or may they be merely evidenced in writing? Alternatively, should a fresh prescribed form always be used? A connected question concerns what, if any, formalities should be observed in order to cancel or rescind a contract which has been made in prescribed form. A possible solution would be to allow parol evidence to prove variation of any terms except the main terms, the variation of these requiring a new form. Similarly, the addition of terms or the cancellation of the contract could be proved by parol evidence except that, again, a prescribed form would have to be used for the main terms of any new contract. Views are requested.

5.28 As with Proposal III, the doctrine of part performance could no longer have any part to play, although other sorts of equitable intervention would remain possible, e.g. on the grounds of proprietary estoppel, misrepresentation, undue influence etc.[41]

5.29 We would like views as to whether solicitors and other qualified practitioners should have implied authority by statute to sign a prescribed form on behalf of a client,[42] or whether an express authority should be necessary. Requiring an express authority could conceivably slow down the transaction, since it would have to be checked, whilst an authority implied by statute, although revocable, could be relied on by anyone not made aware of any revocation However, clients may prefer to sign their own contracts as at present.

Proposal V

5.30 "Cooling-off" periods A statutory provision that the parties to a contract must have time to reconsider (e.g. after an oral agreement reached on the premises or a written contract signed without qualified advice) may on the face of it appear to have some merit. However, "cooling-off" periods are usually associated with contracts entered into under pressure, in circumstances of inequality of bargaining power,[43] which is not as a rule the situation where land is being dealt with[44]. Also, a "cooling-off" period would usually be measured in days, whereas in order to protect consumers, in contracts relating to land, protection would be required up until a time when qualified professional advice can reasonably be sought. Would this additional element of uncertainty, during which neither party knows whether the agreement is to be binding, give rise to unacceptable difficulties in practice, particularly where there is a series of interrelated sales and purchases (i.e. a "chain")?[45] Or would the simplicity of a short "cooling-off" period (eg. five working days) in place of the enduring complexities of the existing legal formalities where house transfers are concerned, be a good idea? The Report of the Expert Committee on Multiple Surveys and Valuations made to the Secretary of State for Scotland in 1984 recommended that a "cooling-off" period should be provided such as that in operation for some land contracts in New South Wales.[46] It is to be remembered, however, that Scotland does not have the problem of chain transactions, and it is instructive to note that the Committee favoured a "cooling-off" period only "in connection with ... new house transactions." If a "cooling-off" period is to be introduced certain important decisions would have to be made: for example when would the period begin? with the making of the contract or, say, only with the first assertion in writing that an oral contract exists? should it be confined to domestic transactions? would it be possible to contract-out of the provision and make an immediate contract? and if so in what circumstances?

PART VI

CONCLUSION

6.1 The Law Commission has not, at this stage, found it necessary to reach any general conclusion or to express a decided preference for any one particular proposal. The present, somewhat tentative, view within the Property Law Team which has prepared this Paper is that there would be advantages, both for the simplification of conveyancing and for the protection of the layman, in the proposal for a type of prescribed form. An illustration of what is in mind is shown on the next page. However, as we have made clear during the discussion of this proposal and the others, no final view has been adopted and there are many aspects of the proposals on which we seek views. It may be that what is required is a range of formalities, from a prescribed form for transactions which are commonly non-commercial, through a requirement of writing for most other transactions, to no formalities at all for others. The details of the proposals have not all been worked out in full. We consider it valuable to seek views on issues of principle before deciding which proposals are worth more detailed consideration. We hope that this paper will give rise to a wide ranging debate on all the possibilities.

Prescribed Form for Contracts for the Sale of Land.

THIS DOCUMENT WHEN COMPLETED IN FULL AND SIGNED MAY CONSTITUTE A BINDING CONTRACT, PROFESSIONAL ADVICE SHOULD BE SOUGHT PRIOR TO SIGNATURE.

CONTRACT FOR SALE made the _______ day of __________________ 19 _____
BETWEEN

PARTIES (1) ________________________

________________________ Vendor(s)

(2) ________________________

________________________ Purchaser(s).

IT IS AGREED that the Vendor(s) will sell as beneficial owner(s) and the Purchaser(s) will buy the Property described at the Price stated and in accordance with the Conditions and Terms made applicable below.

PRICE £ ____

DESCRIPTION OF THE PROPERTY

a) Legal ____

____

b) Physical [a plan may be attached] ______________________

____

c) H.M. Land Registry Title No. [where applicable] ____________

____

STATUTORY CONDITIONS OF SALE

Lord Chancellor's (1985) set to apply except where inconsistent with the following special conditions:- ______________________

____

____

OTHER TERMS (e.g. chattels, repairs) [see schedule on page 2]

Signed (1) ____________________ Witness (if any) (a) ____________

____________________ (address) ____________

(2) ____________________ (b) ____________

6.2 To assist consideration of our various provisional conclusions and proposals, however, we append a precis of them.

(a) The doubts about, and inconsistencies in, the interpretation of section 40 would alone necessitate a reconsideration of its requirements.

(b) There are also difficulties in section 40's interaction with part performance, and the scope of that doctrine itself is now very uncertain.

(c) The need for obtaining legal advice before contracts become binding is recognised, and any reform should neither increase the risks of injustice nor complicate conveyancing.

(d) The proposals were :-

1. To make no change in the law.

2. To repeal section 40 without replacing it.

3. To require all contracts relating to land to be in writing.

4. To require use of a prescribed form. Variations in the form would have to be allowed. Authorisations for signing it may be helpful.

5. To provide for "cooling-off" periods.

Appendix A

Law of Property Act 1925

PART II

CONTRACTS, CONVEYANCES AND OTHER INSTRUMENTS

Contracts

40. Contracts for sale, etc, of land to be in writing

(1) No action may be brought upon any contract for the sale or other disposition of land or any interest in land, unless the agreement upon which such action is brought, or some memorandum or note thereof, is in writing, and signed by the party to be charged or by some other person thereunto by him lawfully authorised.

(2) This section applies to contracts whether made before or after the commencement of this Act and does not affect the law relating to part performance, or sales by the court.

52. (1) All conveyances of land or of any interest therein are void for the purpose of conveying or creating a legal estate unless made by deed.

(2) This section does not apply to-

(a) assents by a personal representative;

(b) disclaimers made in accordance with section fifty-four of the Bankruptcy Act, 1914, or not required to be evidenced in writing;

(c) surrenders by operation of law, including surrenders which may, by law, be effected without writing;

(d) leases or tenancies or other assurances not required by law to be made in writing;

(e) receipts not required by law to be under seal;

(f) vesting orders of the court or other competent authority;

(g) conveyances taking effect by operation of law.

53. (1) Subject to the provision hereinafter contained with respect to the creation of interests in land by parol-

(a) no interest inland can be created or disposed of except by writing signed by the person creating or conveying the same, or by his agent thereunto lawfully authorised in writing, or by will, or by operation of law;

(b) a declaration of trust respecting any land or any interest therein must be manifested and proved by some writing signed by some person who is able to declare such trust or by his will;

(c) a disposition of an equitable interest or trust subsisting at the time of the disposition, must be in writing signed by the person disposing of the same, or by his agent thereunto lawfully authorised in writing or by will.

(2) This section does not affect the creation or operation of resulting, implied or constructive trusts.

54 (1) All interests in land created by parol and not put in writing and signed by the persons so creating the same, or by their agents thereunto lawfully authorised in writing, have, notwithstanding any consideration having been given for the same, the force and effect of interests at will only.

(2) Nothing in the foregoing provisions of this Part of this Act shall affect the creation by parol of leases taking effect in possession for a term not exceeding three years (whether or not the lessee is given power to extend the term) at the best rent which can be reasonable obtained without taking a fine.

55. Nothing in the foregoing sections shall-

(a) invalidate dispositions by will; or

(b) affect any interest validly created before the commencement of this Act; or

(c) affect the right to acquire an interest in land by virtue of taking possession; or

(d) affect the operation of the law relating to part performance.

205. (1) In this Act unless the context otherwise requires, the following expressions have the meanings hereby assigned to them respectively, that is to say:-

(ii) "Conveyance" includes a mortgage, charge, lease, assent, vesting declaration, vesting instrument, disclaimer, release and every other assurance of property or of an interest therein by any instrument, except a will; "convey" has a corresponding meaning; and "disposition" includes a conveyance and also a devise, bequest, or an appointment of property contained in a will; and "dispose of" has a corresponding meaning;

(v) "Estate owner" means the owner of a legal estate, but an infant is not capable of being an estate owner;

(ix) "Land" includes land of any tenure, and mines and minerals, whether or not held apart from the surface, buildings or parts of buildings (whether the division is horizontal, vertical or made in any other way) and other corporeal hereditaments; also a manor, an advowson, and a rent and other incorporeal hereditaments, and an easement, right, privilege, or benefit in, over, or derived from land; but not an undivided share in land; and "mines and minerals" include any strata or seam of minerals or substances in or under any land,

and powers of working and getting the same but not an undivided share thereof; and "manor" includes a lordship, and reputed manor or lordship; and "hereditament' means any real property which on an intestacy occurring before the commencement of this Act might have devolved upon an heir;

(x) "Legal estates" mean the estates, interests and charges, in or over land (subsisting or created at law) which are by this Act authorised to subsist or to be created a legal estates; "equitable interests" mean all the other interests and charges in or over land or in the proceeds of sale thereof; an equitable interest "capable of subsisting as a legal estate" means such as could validly subsist or be created as a legal estate under this Act;

(xxiv) "Sale" includes an extinguishment of manorial incidents, but inother respects means a sale properly so called;)

Appendix B

Law v. Jones [1974] Ch. 112 (Court of Appeal)

The plaintiff and defendant reached an oral agreement that the defendant would sell his cottage to the plaintiff for £6,500. The defendant's solicitors wrote to the plaintiff's solicitors concerning the plaintiff's "proposed purchase" of the property for £6,500 "subject to contact". The letter did not identify the vendor. A few days later, they wrote again, with a draft contract which contained all the essential terms. The plaintiff's solicitors acknowledged both letters. The parties then reached an oral agreement which it was clear was intended to be binding, that the price should be increased by £500. The defendant's solicitors wrote to the plaintiff's solicitors referring to the agreed increase and asking them to amend the draft contract. That letter did not say "subject to contract". The defendant refused to complete the sale of the cottage, and the plaintiff claimed specific performance.

It was held (Russell L.J. dissenting) that there was a new enforceable contract. The letter confirming the agreed increase together with the other documents to which it was linked contained the essential terms of the new contract agreed by the parties when they agreed the increase in price. To satisfy section 40 a memorandum did not have to acknowledge the existence of a contract, although it must not deny the existence of a contract.

Tiverton Estates Ltd. v. Wearwell Ltd. [1975] Ch. 146 (Court of Appeal)

A director of the plaintiff company, which owned a property, orally agreed to sell it to the defendant company. The defendant's solicitor wrote to the plaintiff's solicitor concerning the "proposed sale of the ... property ... at £190,000 leasehold subject to contract...". The plaintiff's solicitor acknowledged receipt and sent a draft contract. The plaintiff then decided not to sell. The defendant's solicitor lodged a caution at the Land Registry. The plaintiff brought proceedings to have the caution vacated and the defendant brought a counterclaim for specific performance.

It was held that a memorandum, in order to satisfy section 40, must contain an acknowledgment or recognition that a contract has been entered into and that the words "subject to contract" in the defendant's solicitor's letter showed that no contract was acknowledged.

FOOTNOTES TO PART I INTRODUCTION

1 The section is set out in full at Appendix A.

2 [1974] Ch. 112, and see Appendix B for a brief account.

3 See A.M. Prichard (1974) 90 L.Q.R. 55 at p. 71, "It is a decision that piquantly finds Russell L.J. dissenting for fear that it would have disastrous effects upon conveyancing practice. Certainly this fear has been speedily shared by conveyancers, led by the learned Editor of the Solicitors' Journal" (e.g. (1973) 117 S.J. 293).

4 [1975] Ch. 146, and see Appendix B for a brief account.

5 Unpublished

6 [1974] Ch. 112.

7 [1975] Ch. 146.

8 E.g. per Harman J. in Burgess v. Cox [1951] Ch. 383 at p. 388, the Statute of Frauds, s. 4 and s. 40 have been "under judicial fire for over two centuries"; also per Stamp J. in Wakeham v. Mackenzie [1968] 1 W.L.R. 1175 at p. 1178; H.W. Wilkinson (1967) 31 Conv. (N.S.) 182 and 254; Barnsley's Conveyancing Law and Practice 2nd ed., (1982), p. 102. Cf. Scarman L.J. in Steadman v. Steadman [1974] Q.B. 161 at p. 184 where he said that there was no strong pressure for the repeal of s. 40. But see also M.P. Thompson [1983] Conv. 78 in a case note on Elias v. George Sahely [1983] 1 A.C. 646, "Cases appear with almost monotonous regularity concerning the requirements of this troublesome section".

9 A.M. Prichard, "An aspect of contracts and their terms", (1974) 90 L.Q.R. 55 at p. 78.

10 Paras. 7.4-7.6 as follows:,

"**Contracts in Writing**

7.4 The formalities which must be complied with in order for a contract for the transfer (whether by way of sale or lease) of a house or flat to be enforceable are prescribed by s.40(1) of the Law of Property Act 1925:

> "No action may be brought upon any contract for the sale or other disposition of land or any interest in land, unless the agreement upon which such action is brought, or some memorandum or note thereof, is in writing, and signed by the party to be charged or by some other person thereunto by him lawfully authorised."

7.5 This statutory provision, originally designed to prevent fraud occurring because of conflicts of oral evidence, has appeared in practice to be used most often to defeat what would otherwise be entirely valid contracts. The doctrine of part-performance developed by the courts so that the provision itself should not be used as an instrument of fraud (statutorily recognised in the Law of Property Act 1925, s.40(2)) could now be regarded as having undermined the requirement of written evidence, with the result that it has become substantially meaningless. The operation of the provision in relation to letters following an oral agreement but headed 'subject to contract' has caused excessive concern to practitioners. The need to evidence all the terms actually agreed, even those relating to repairs or chattels, together with the possibilities of waiver or submission in relation to omitted terms and of the joinder of the documents to create a memorandum have given rise to unacceptable complications and uncertainties. Submissions from the Society for Public Teachers of Law commented that "The complexity of the rules that have grown up round section 40 of the Law of Property Act 1925 is disgraceful". In addition the application of the provision, especially as to signatures, where contracts are negotiated and concluded by electronic communications between solicitors or other conveyancers might lead to further litigation. A multitude of nice academic but bad practical problems can be derived from s.40.

7.6 The submissions received by us have varied between two extremes: on the one hand, the simple repeal of s.40 has been urged so that an oral sale of land would simply become enforceable; on the other hand, amendment of the section has been commended with the object that such contracts must always be made by some formal writing, so that mere written evidence of an oral agreement would never suffice. Strong support for the latter suggestion may be seen in two factors: first, in conveyancing practice at present almost all contracts for the sale and purchase of land are made in writing using standard forms (i.e. exchange of parts incorporating The Law Society's or the National Conditions of Sale). Second, the basic proposition made at paragraph 1.35 of our First Report that "Buying a property represents for many people the most important financial transaction of their lives" leads also to the conclusion that informality and uncertainty are undesirable."

See further para. 5.19 of this present paper as to the Committee's suggested solution of a prescribed form.

FOOTNOTES TO PART II

1 For a detailed commentary see Emmet on Title 18th ed., (1983) chap. 2, parts 1, 2 and 3; Williams on Title 4th ed., (1975) chap. 2.

2 See Preamble, also Lord Wright, Legal Essays and Addresses, (1939), p. 226.

3 See Wolstenholme & Cherry's Conveyancing Statutes 13th ed., (1972) vol. 1, p. 101.

4 By the Law Reform (Enforcement of Contracts) Act 1954.

5 (1937), Cmd. 5449: reprinted 1951.

6 H.W. Wilkinson (1967) 31 Conv. (N.S.) 182.

7 Barnsley's Conveyancing Law and Practice 2nd ed., (1982), p. 102.

8 See Appendix A.

9 [1955] Ch. 431.

10 Jenkins L.J. ibid, at p. 439 was of the opinion that the definition in s. 205(1)(ix) of the L.P.A. 1925 did not conclude the matter as the interest in question was a right to share in the proceeds to arise from a sale of land rather than an undivided share and since s. 40 replaces s. 4 of the Statute of Frauds 1677 which in his view would have covered such an interest, he was reluctant to construe s. 40 so as not to. See also Steadman v Steadman [1974] Q.B. 161 at p. 167.

11 The definition section (s. 205(1)(ii)) of the L.P.A. 1925 provides that:

> "'Conveyance' includes a mortgage, charge, lease, assent, vesting declaration, vesting instrument, disclaimer, release and every

other assurance of property or of an interest therein by any instrument, except a will; 'convey' has a corresponding meaning; and 'disposition' includes a conveyance and also a devise, bequest, or an appointment of property contained in a will; and 'dispose of' has a corresponding meaning;"

12 Law v. Jones [1974] Ch. 112; Tiverton Estates Ltd. v. Wearwell [1975] Ch. 146; and compare Barnsley op. cit. at p. 102, "All that the statute requires is the existence of a written note or memorandum evidencing the terms of the agreement" (emphasis in original) with Cheshire and Burn, Modern Law of Real Property 13th ed., (1982), p. 112 where it is stated that the section also requires "an express or implied recognition that a contract was actually entered into".

13 Potter v. Duffield (1874) L.R. 18 Eq. 4.

14 Davies v. Sweet [1962] 2 Q.B. 300.

15 A reasonable price will not be implied, but an agreement to sell at a "reasonable price" may be sufficiently ascertainable as a court can decide what is a fair price. See Sudbrook Trading Estate Ltd v. Eggleton [1983] 1 A.C. 444.

16 Hawkins v. Price [1947] Ch. 645.

17 Hill v. Hill [1947] Ch. 231.

18 Timmins v. Moreland Street Property Co. Ltd [1958] Ch. 110; Elias v. George Sahely & Co (Barbados) Ltd. [1983] 1 A.C. 646 P.C.

19 Hill v. Hill [1947] Ch. 231.

20 Monnickendam v. Leanse (1923) 39 T.L.R. 445; Low v. Fry (1935) 51 T.L.R. 322; cp. Chillingworth v. Esche [1924] 1 Ch. 97, also Pulbrook v. Lawes (1876) 1 Q.B.D. 284, as to recovery of a deposit by a purchaser where a vendor defaults. For the

possibility that payment of a deposit may be a sufficient act of part performance to make the contract enforceable by the purchaser, see Steadman v. Steadman [1976] A.C. 536 (para. 2.14 below).

21 Leroux v Brown (1852) 12 C.B. 801.

22 But see Williams on Title 4th ed., (1975), p. 78 where it is still stated that the acts must be unequivocal. Compare this with Cheshire and Burn, Modern Law of Real Property 13th ed., (1982) p. 119 where it is stated that the strict unequivocal rule has been modified by Kingswood Estate Co. Ltd. v. Anderson [1963] 2 Q.B. 169.

23 Steadman v. Steadman [1976] A.C. 536 at p. 564, per Lord Simon of Glaisdale.

24 Biss v. Hygate [1918] 2 K.B. 314 at p. 317 per Lawrence J.

25 Turner v. Melladew (1903) 19 T.L.R. 273.

26 [1976] A.C. 536.

27 See on this point Emmet on Title 18th ed., (1983), p. 69.

28 [1979] Ch. 16.

29 See M.P. Thompson "The role of evidence in part performance", [1979] Conv. 402, where it is argued that this so-called rule has never been a part of the law, except when the views of Warrington L.J. [in Chaproniere v. Lambert [1917] 2 Ch. 356] held sway, and that the opinion of Lord Reid in the Steadman case was in line with the law as it had developed.

30 Steadman v. Steadman [1976] A.C. 536, per Lord Salmon at p. 570.

31 Cp. n. 22 above.

FOOTNOTES TO PART III

1 See above para. 2.3.

2 See H.W. Wilkinson at (1967) 31 Conv. (N.S.) 182.

3 See Report (1937), Cmd. 5449 para. 9.

4 See above para. 2.2.

5 It is a well-known practice nowadays to exchange formal written contracts yet it may still not be uncommon that an oral agreement is reached by lay parties on the property in which case the criticism would apply (see, e.g., Farrell v. Green (1974) 232 E.G. 587).

6 [1918] A.C. 1.

7 This was a result which the parties "could not possibly have intended". Note that had the consequence of failure to comply with the statute been invalidity instead of unenforceability, the earlier contract would have remained valid and enforceable, which would also have been an unintended result: cp. United Dominions Corporation Ltd v. Shoucair [1969] 1 A.C. 340.

8 See A.M. Prichard "An aspect of contracts and their terms" (1974) 90 L.Q.R. 55 at p. 65.

9 [1974] Ch. 112 and see Appendix B.

10 Buckley L.J. at p. 126.

11 [1975] Ch. 146 and see Appendix B.

12 Per Buckley L.J. (one of the Law v. Jones majority) in Daulia Ltd. v. Four Millbank Nominees Ltd. [1978] Ch. 231 at p. 250.

13 E.g. C.T. Emery, "The alarm bell continues to ring", [1974] C.L.J. 42; Emmet on Title 18th ed., (1983), p. 48; M.J. Perry "S. 40 of the Law of Property Act 1925 and 'Subject to Contract'", (1974) 71 L.S. Gaz. 340; R. Clark, "'Subject to contract' I, English problems," [1984] Conv. 173.

14 J.C.W. Wylie, Irish Conveyancing Law (1978) p. 342, "After considerable controversy, the English courts seem to have reached the conclusion that such a qualification ['subject to contract'] in the alleged memorandum, by negativing the existence of an agreement between the parties, renders it insufficient". Footnotes omitted. Also Ruoff and Roper, Registered Conveyancing 4th ed., (1979), p. 304, "For the purposes of this section [s. 40] a memorandum or note must not only state the terms of the contract but must also contain an acknowledgement or recognition by the signatory to the document that a contract has been entered into". Tiverton is cited as authority for this statement with no mention in the whole book of Law v. Jones. Also Cheshire and Burn, Modern Law of Real Property 13th ed., (1982), pp. 112-113 where Tiverton is accepted and Law v. Jones is relegated to a footnote.

15 [1974] Ch. 112 at p. 125.

16 Cp. Alpenstow Ltd. v. Regalian Properties Plc. [1985] 1 W.L.R. 721, where the words "subject to contract" were used in an agent's letter of offer; Nourse J. held that, in the exceptional context, an acceptance by letter constituted a contract despite those words; no reliance was placed on the Tiverton case as authority for the contract not being enforceable because of an insuffiicent memorandum.

17 See above para. 1.4.

18 Cooper v. Critchley [1955] Ch. 431; see also para. 2.5 and n. 10.

19 Irani Finance Ltd v. Singh [1971] Ch. 59.

20 [1976] A.C. 536 and [1974] 1 Q.B. 161.

21 Driver v. Broad [1893] 1 Q.B. 744.

22 Webber v. Lee (1882) 9 Q.B.D. 315.

23 Cp. Morgan v. Russell & Sons [1909] 1 K.B. 357; see also s. 61(1) of the Sale of Goods Act 1979 where "goods" are defined as:

> "all personal chattels other than things in action and money, and in Scotland all corporeal moveables except money; and in particular 'goods' includes emblements, industrial growing crops, and things attached to or forming part of the land which are agreed to be severed before sale or under the contract of sale;"

24 Compare for example the case of E.R. Ives Investment Ltd. v. High [1967] 2 Q.B. 379 with that of National Provincial Bank Ltd. v. Ainsworth [1965] A.C. 1175.

25 See G. Fridman "Joinder of documents to form a memorandum", (1958) 22 Conv. (N.S.) 275.

26 The provision reads "In any Act, unless the contrary intention appears,- ... (c) words in the singular include the plural and words in the plural include the singular"; s. 6 of the Interpretation Act 1978. This was a consolidating statute but, for present purposes, this provision only applies to Acts passed after 1850 (ss. 22(1) and 23(1) and Sched. 2, para. 2). Accordingly neither it nor its predecessor could govern the construction of the Statute of Frauds 1677 (which was consolidated in part into s. 40 of the 1925 Act: see as to construction Cooper v. Critchley [1955] Ch. 431). The joinder of documents rule was applied long before the 1925 consolidation: see, e.g. Boydell v. Drummond (1809) 11 East. 142.

27 Long v. Millar (1879) 4 C.P.D. 450 which gave a more liberal interpretation of the rule than that laid down in the earlier case of Peirce v. Corf (1874) L.R. 9 Q.B. 210.

28 Sheers v. Thimbleby & Son (1897) 76 L.T. 709.

29 Burgess v. Cox [1951] Ch. 383.

30 [1958] Ch. 110, 130-131.

31 [1983] 1 A.C. 646 at p. 655.

32 F. Goldsmith (Sicklesmere) Ltd v. Baxter [1970] Ch. 85.

33 Auerbach v. Nelson [1919] 2 Ch. 383 per Astbury J. at p. 388.

34 [1916] 2 Ch. 233.

35 [1962] 2 Q.B. 300, 308.

36 Basma v. Weekes [1950] A.C. 441.

37 [1897] 2 Ch. 281.

38 Auerbach v. Nelson [1919] 2 Ch. 383.

39 Timmins v. Moreland Street Property Co. Ltd [1958] Ch. 110.

40 Ibid., per Romer L.J. at p. 132.

41 Gourlay v. Somerset (1815) 19 Ves. 429.

42 Leeman v. Stocks [1951] Ch. 941.

43 Hubert v. Treherne (1842) 3 Man. & G. 743.

44 See, for example, Leeman v. Stocks, ibid.

45 New Hart Builders Ltd v. Brindley [1975] Ch. 342.

46 C.T. Emery "Statute of Frauds: The authenticated signature fiction - an illogicial distinction" (1975) 39 Conv. (N.S.) 336.

47 Smith v. Wheatcroft (1878) 9 Ch.D. 223. Note that implied terms need not be evidenced in writing, also as with all contracts rectification may be available.

48 Hawkins v. Price [1947] Ch. 645.

49 4th ed., (1936) vol 1, p. 5.

50 (1852) 22 L.J. Ch. 94.

51 [1951] Ch. 383.

52 [1971] 1 Ch. 850.

53 Barnsley op. cit., at p. 102.

54 Barnsley op. cit. at p. 119.

55 [1976] A.C. 536.

56 Followed as to this in Re Windle [1975] 1 W.L.R. 1628.

57 See a note at (1974) 38 Conv. (N.S.) 388-391.

58 M.P. Thompson "The role of evidence in part performance", [1979] Conv. 402 at p. 413.

59 Steadman v. Steadman [1976] A.C. 536 at p. 542 per Lord Reid, p. 562 per Lord Simon of Glaisdale.

60 [1979] Ch. 16.

61 M.P. Thompson "The role of evidence in part performance", [1979] Conv. 402.

FOOTNOTES TO PART IV

1 This proposal was put forward in a letter to the Commission from the Council of The Law Society.

2 A.M. Prichard, "An aspect of contracts and their terms", (1974) 90 L.Q.R. 55.

3 See e.g. D.W. McLauchlan, The Parol Evidence Rule (1976) N.Z., chap. 4.

4 By The Law Society's Land Law and Conveyancing Committee (post-Tiverton).

5 Thirkell v. Cambi [1919] 2 K.B. 590; Horner v. Walker [1923] 2 Ch. 218.

6 The requirement that an agent signing should be so authorised in writing may already be seen in ss. 53(1) and 54(1) of the L.P.A. 1925, which provisions also derive from the Statute of Frauds 1677.

7 Cmd. 5449 and see above para. 3.2.

8 H.W. Wilkinson, "Law of Property Act 1925, s. 40: a case for amendment", (1967) 31 Conv. (N.S.) 254; see also Second Interim Report of The Law Society's Working Party on Conveyancing (1966) 63 L.S. Gaz. 171.

FOOTNOTES TO PART V

1 Five major professional societies, The Law Society, the Royal Institution of Chartered Surveyors, the Chartered Land Agents' Society, the Chartered Auctioneers and Estate Agents' Institute and the Incorporated Society of Auctioneers and Landed Property Agents, have in the past expressed this view (1966) 63 L. S. Gaz. 267, as has the Law Commission, Law Com. No. 65, p. 4.

2 Section 52 requires conveyances of legal estates to be by deed whilst ss. 53 and 54 are directed against the creation or disposition of any interest in land without signed writing.

3 See Goff & Jones The Law of Restitution 2nd ed., (1978), p. 297 et seq. as to "Ineffective Transactions".

4 Cp. Bradford Advance Co. Ltd. v. Ayers [1924] WN 152 and North Central Wagon Finance Co. Ltd. v. Brailsford [1962] 1 W.L.R. 1288 concerning void bills of sale where money advanced was held recoverable with interest at a reasonable rate.

5 Cp. Brewer Street Investments Ltd. v. Barclays Woollen Co. Ltd. [1954] 1 Q.B. 428 C.A. where a prospective landlord who had had work done to the prospective tenants' specification was reimbursed. In argument in that case, also, Romer L.J. said (at p. 431):

> "Suppose that, whilst parties were in negotiation for a lease, the landlord allowed the prospective tenants to go on the land and spend money on it in anticipation of a lease. If the landlords subsequently broke off negotiations for no reason at all they could not get the benefit of the work without paying for it. Equity would give a remedy".

Denning L.J. added (ibid):

> "Whether equity would do so or not, the common law, nowadays, would give the prospective tenants the right to recover the value of the work done in an action for restitution".

6 See Snell Principles of Equity (Baker and Langan) 28th ed., (1982), pp. 554-563. Especial reference may be made to the observations of Lord Denning M.R. in Amalgamated Investment & Property Co. Ltd. v. Texas Commerce International Bank Ltd. [1982] Q.B. 84 at p. 122:

> "The doctrine of estoppel is one of the most flexible and useful in the armoury of the law. But it has become overloaded with cases. That is why I have not gone through them all in this judgment. It has evolved during the last 150 years in a sequence of separate developments: proprietary estoppel, estoppel by representation of fact, estoppel by acquiescence, and promissory estoppel. At the same time it has been sought to be limited by a series of maxims: estoppel is only a rule of evidence, estoppel cannot give rise to a cause of action, estoppel cannot do away with the need for consideration, and so forth. All these can now be seen to merge into one general principle shorn of limitations. When the parties to a transaction proceed on the basis of an underlying assumption - either of fact or of law - and whether due to misrepresentation or mistake makes no difference - on which they have conducted the dealings between them - neither of them will be allowed to go back on that assumption when it would be unfair or unjust to allow him to do so. If one of them does seek to go back on it, the courts will give the other such remedy as the equity of the case demands."

See also notes at [1983] Conv. 85-87 and [1984] Conv. 1-2.

7 See not only Snell, loc. cit. but also Goff & Jones, op. cit. at p. 110.

8 See per Pennycuick V.-C. in Damm v. Herrtage (1974) 234 E.G. 365 at p. 371 but cp. the same learned judge in Farrell v. Green (1974) 232 E.G. 587.

9 See, e.g. ss. 53(1) and 54(1) of L.P.A. 1925.

10 That is leases for 3 years or less within s. 54(2) of the L.P.A. 1925.

11 See above para. 1.8.

12 Cp. s. 53(1)(c) of the L.P.A. 1925 which has been held to apply to a contract to assign an equitable interest: Oughtred v. IRC [1960] A.C. 206.

13 See Land Charges Act 1972 s. 2(4)(iv), also Land Registration Act 1925, s. 59.

14 See s. 17(1) of the 1972 Act and ss. 1(1) and 205(1)(x) of the L.P.A. 1925.

15 Cp. s. 54(2) of the Law of Property Act 1925; also s.52(2) of the same Act as to conveyances of legal estates which do not have to be by deed.

16 See Midland Bank Trust Co. Ltd. v. Green [1981] A.C. 513 at p. 531 where Lord Wilberforce confirmed that the case of Re Monolithic Building Co. [1915] 1 Ch. 643 "makes it clear that it is not 'fraud' to rely on legal rights conferred by Act of Parliament".

17 See para. 5.8 above.

18 See L.P.A. 1925, ss. 53 and 54; these apply particularly to the creation of equitable interests in land and a specifically enforceable contract for sale operates to vest such an interest in the purchaser but by virtue of the vendor's constructive trusteeship: Rayner v. Preston (1881) 18 Ch. D. 1; constructive trusts are expressly outside s. 53, but not s. 54, of the 1925 Act.

19 The Law Commission is currently considering the issue of the admissibility of parol evidence (see Law Com. Working Paper No. 70).

20 Cp. Harvey v. Pratt [1965] 1 W.L.R. 1025.

21 Cp. Parker v. Clark [1960] 1 W.L.R. 286; see also per Buckley L.J. in Daulia Ltd. v. Four Millbank Nominees Ltd. [1978] Ch. 231 at p. 250 as to a new oral agreement being evidenced by an earlier letter.

22 See Stearn v. Twitchell [1985] 1 All E.R. 631.

23 So decided in relation to s. 53(1)(c) of the L.P.A. 1925 by Megarry J. in Re Danish Bacon Co. Ltd. Staff Pension Fund Trusts [1971] 1 W.L.R. 248.

24 See ss. 53(1) and 54(1) of the L.P.A. 1925.

25 As in the previously cited provisions.

26 Cp. as to conditions void by statute listed in Emmet on Title 18th ed., (1983), at pp. 71-72.

27 Hire Purchase Act, 1965, ss. 5 and 7 and see now Consumer Credit Act 1974, s. 61 and the regulations made under it (S.I. 1983/1553).

28 Protection from Eviction Act 1977, s. 5.

29 See Land Registration Rules 1925, r. 74 and Sched.

30 (1985), Chairman: Professor Julian Farrand, para. 9.36, and see paras. 7.4-7.11.

31 Cp. notes already heading The Law Society's Contract for Sale Form (1984): "IMPORTANT This is a technical document, designed to create specific legal rights and obligations. It is recommended for use only in accordance with the advice of your solicitors." There is an equivalent note at the foot of the National Form.

32 For the current version see Emmet on Title 18th ed., (1983), at pp. 83-86.

33 [1985] 1 All E.R. 631.

34 (1984), para. 1.22. While many of the recommendations of the Report are embodied in the Administration of Justice Bill 1985, the Bill itself does not restrict licensed conveyancers to domestic conveyancing.

35 Which themselves have to be in writing, s. 53(1)(c) of the L.P.A. 1925.

36 Cp. Housing Act 1980, s. 55(2).

37 Land Registration Rules 1925, r. 98 and Sched., Form 19 at seq.

38 As in Smith v. Mansi [1963] 1 W.L.R. 26.

39 Cp. Alpenstow Ltd. v. Regalian Properties Plc. [1985] 1 W.L.R. 721.

40 See Property and Bloodstock Ltd. v. Emerton [1967] 2 All E.R. 839 and [1968] Ch. 94.

41 See para. 5.8.

42 At present solicitors have implied authority to sign a memorandum evidencing a contract, but no implied authority to make a contract (but compare the position in Scotland). Any agent who acts without authority may, however, be sued for breach of warranty of authority: cp. V/O Rasnoimport v. Guthrie & Co Ltd [1966] 1 Lloyd's Rep. 1.

43 Cp. Consumer Credit Act 1974, ss. 67-73.

44 But see Pateman v. Pay (1974) 232 E.G. 457 and Damm v. Herrtage (1974) 234 E.G. 365 in each of which potential purchasers were anxious to avoid any risk of gazumping and adopted devices which could be stigmatised as "sharp practice".

45 Cp. The Conveyancing Supplement to S.J. 19 April 1985 at p. 11.

46 Land Vendors Act 1964, as amended; this provision has been described as "ill-conceived, badly expressed and badly implemented", conferring "almost no practical benefit on its consumers" Lang N.S.W. Conveyancing Law and Practice (1980), vol. 1, para. 5-700.

Printed in the UK for HMSO
Dd 738597 C17 9/85